Through My Eyes

Kayleen Oftedal

BookLeaf Publishing

Presentation by *BookLeaf Publishing*

Web: www.bookleafpub.com

E-mail: info@bookleafpub.com

ISBN: 9789357212991

First edition 2023

To all the lights that guide me home

PREFACE

I hope that the people who read this will be able to relate these feelings and sentiments to people in their own lives. By reading this book, I hope they will be made more aware of the little things they appreciate about each person.

January 4

She is dark band t-shirts
At home hair cuts
Specially made interior designs
And the stomp of line dancing at bars
She is the shine of a silver dress
The taste of goat milk coffee
The glint of the stars meant for dancing under
And a little ladybug cup
She is made for rock climbing
Giggling about boys
Driving a car with eyelashes named Helga
And being the best waitress around

February 5

She is late-night walks by the river
Cringey videos made as kids
The sound of piano music in the sanctuary
And the taste of a half-eaten birthday cake
She is the feeling of reading a comfort book on a
cold winter day
Sharing desserts at church potlucks
The smell of freshly fallen rain
And the look of a navy blue dress under
Christmas lights
She is made for singing soprano in the choir
Sending letters to each other
Gossiping over freshly poured coffee
And having the darkest sense of humour

March 1

She is the smell of freshly tilled dirt in the spring
The taste of homemade buns straight out of the
oven
The glow of lights on a Charlie Brown
Christmas tree
And feel of grass beneath my back while cloud
gazing
She is the taste of hot chocolate made just right
A white and blue color scheme
The feeling of finishing a large puzzle
And the colorful sunset peeking through the
trees
She is made for teaching me how to cross stitch
Staining the deck on a hot summer day
Tea with a little bit of honey in the evening
And playing Bananagrams after breakfast

March 16

She is the taste of cheesecake from a long-closed
eatery
The feel of a fuzzy blanket in a cold hockey rink
The taste of homemade bread and jam
And the most beautiful bride to be found
She is the feeling of walking around Christmas
craft sales
The smell of cinnamon and brown sugar
The fun of working at camp through the summer
And the giggle after a shared inside joke
She is made for ignoring work to have small
chats
Evening discussions over fruit punch and
mashed potatoes
Singing in the church worship team
And giving the best hugs

March 20

She is the taste of raspberry cake at an evening
party
The feel of rollerskating behind a bike
Late night storytelling
And friendship at the first meeting
She is a warm fire on a rainy day
A goofy smile after a silly joke
Sharing water on hot summer days
And care packages sent from Switzerland
She is made for bouldering
Drunken word games late into the night
Riding bikes around Home Hardware
And amazing baking skills

April 1

She is the beauty of a top-floor garden
The comfort of an old wool sweater
The crinkle of wrapping paper on Christmas
morning
And the taste of iced capps from Tim Hortons
She is the lights from the festival at the zoo
The beat of square dancing at the Calgary
Stampede
Going to the beach without towels
And wonder of skating on a pond under city
lights
She is made for speaking her mind
Sitting on rocks and looking down at the city
Having a cat that always likes her roommate
better
And endless photoshoots in the mountain

April 6

She is ice cream and Supernatural over lunch
break
The feel of dancing at my first Halloween party
Late-night phone calls to keep me company
And shared clothing after sleepovers
She is the taste powdered donuts while kayaking
The feel of fresh air while jogging in the
morning
Dropping an egg off the balcony
And watching The Emperor's New Groove for
the first time
She is made for afternoon art classes
Sorting calves on a cloudy May morning
Driving around in her old beater
And flying helicopters over cities

May 26

He is the burn of biking to the power station
The tickle of whisker rubs on my cheek before
bed
The softness of a well-worn sweater
And the smell of Old spice and aftershave
He is the taste of a dark chocolate orange
The sleepiness of driving home from late hockey
practices
Sharing the same sense of humor
And the sound of music from the 80s
He is made for dancing weirdly around the
kitchen
Yearly movie marathons of Lord of the Rings
Early morning pancakes on Sundays
And taking the dog for walks around the yard

June 11

She is the feeling of riding horses to get the mail
The sound of Disney sing-alongs during car
rides
The taste of freshly made cookie dough
And the glow of tree lights on Christmas
morning
She is the feeling of mountain camping in the
snow
The sound of leaves crunching underfoot
The taste of homemade sandwiches during
picnics in the yard
And the wonder of sitting on the roof to look at
the stars
She is made for watching The Sword in the
Stone after weddings
Teaching me how to swing dance
Inchworm races over river ice
And random check-in phone calls throughout the
day

June 22

He is the sound of laughter from dumb bus ride
jokes
The smell of hay and manure on the farm
The feeling of skating on the dugout during a
crisp winter night
And the taste of warm cinnamon buns right out
of the oven
He is the feeling of a worn flannel shirt
Snowmobiling around the field with a sled
behind
The smell of diesel and engine grease
And the fun of playing kick the can in the
evening
He is made for growing up together
Playing piano duets in the auditorium
Being my grad escort
And my unintentional twin and brother

July 1

She is the taste of candy canes at Christmas
The feeling of cheering on the soccer team in the
rain
Dancing in our comfy pajamas
And the smell of fresh flowers on a spring
morning
She is the joy of old-time dancing at the activity
center
Doing homework together after school
The laughter after watching a Twilight spin-off
And the most uplifting personality I know
She is made for late-night 7/11 runs
Playing volleyball together
Visiting at work with a McDonald's frappe and
gossip
And being the Goose to my Maverick

July 6

She is the sound of whispers in the library
The taste of Tim Horton's farmer's wraps after
class
Chats about music on the way home
And laughing about the word 'tryptophane'
She is the taste of coffee much needed to stay
awake
The giggles over the punch wind up
A much-needed coincidental meeting
And pictures of her orange cat Luther
She is made for warm jacket to keep away the
cold
Hair clips that keep her hair out of her face
Comfy sweats for evening classes
And walking from library to library in search of
a place to study

July 11

She is the promise of star spinning
The taste of beaver tails in the capital
The wonder of exploring museums and art
galleries
And the sound of karaoke at talent nights
She is the color green
Nutella and peanut butter on toast
Where the mountains meet the sea
And daisy crowns made in summer
She is made for dressing up as Marty McFly
Always carrying around her camera
Video updates to brighten up my day
And never-ending promises to see each other
soon

July 31

She is the taste of Wendy's after Monday night
classes
The feel of watching Cheers after a day of
studying
Random runs to Walmart late at night
And movie nights on campus
She is the feeling of getting lost in buildings
The taste of ice cream and pizza at a sleepover
The feel of a well-worn sweater on a cool
evening
And the smell of a spice-scented candle
She is made for studying adolescent psychology
Fun nights out at the bar
Talking about her summers at the lake
And mushroom swiss burgers from Sunny Side
bar

August 18

She is the feel of yarn between my fingers
The taste of homemade chocolate milkshakes on
movie nights
The smell of the forest during a long summer
hike
And the steam coming off freshly brewed tea
She is the sunflowers reaching for the sky
The reassuring hug after a bad day
The shared laughter around the fire
And driving to Battleford to get her new car
She is made for bookshelves and knick-knacks
Cuddling and watching Barbie movies
Being the best cat mom
And sharing childhood memories

August 22

She is the feeling of running to the aqua jog in
the evening
Inside jokes to laugh at
The burn of chopping wood at the shack
And the taste of homemade espresso ice cream
She is the sound of Swiss in the house
The feeling of lying in the pool on a hot
summers day
The freedom of the cotton eyed joe
And the comfort of sleepy mornings
She is made for loving cheese
Team marathons in the mountains
Rollerblading around the lake
And road trips in a beat-up van

September 29

She is the taste of fritters on a cold winter
evening
The comfort of a hug after being apart for so
long
The feel of fuzzy socks on a snowy day
And the smell of fresh monkey bread
She is the chill of sitting in a cold hockey rink
watching my cousin play
The laughter at a Christmas concert play
The sound of songs from the choir
And the cheer of someone who is always in my
corner
She is made for dropping into my work just to
say hi
Being the aunt to my entire elementary school
Watching Judge Judy and visiting
And calling me Dumplin'

October 10

He is the smell of cigar smoke around the fire
A shared sweater on a drizzly night
Dancing at music festivals
And the soft touch of holding bunnies for the
first time
He is joking around the card table
Dressing up as John Lennon for Halloween
The feel of fresh mountain air
And the triumph of running a solo marathon
He is made for taekwondo
Losing at ladder ball
Hiking with his family in the mountains
And swimming in frigid lakes after a long day of
running

November 15

She is the glow from a jack-o'lantern on
Halloween
The taste of pasta on Wednesdays after
volleyball
The feel of head scratches after a long day
And the comfort of a much-needed nap
She is homemade red velvet cakes
New nail designs for me to admire
The comfort of a home-designed travel cup
And the sound of laughter after an inside joke
She is made for movie nights and wine
Decorating her house for every major holiday
Hockey nights watching her son
And long walks through the dog park in the fall

December 7

He is random facts about the weirdest topics
The feel of watching Demon Slayer after school
The taste of homemade chocolate milk
And TikTok dances with his cousin
He is last minute plans for the movie theatre
Arcade games and over-buttered popcorn
Going to the mall for anime stickers
And afternoon drives to the art store
He is made for cuddling his puppies
Showing me how to play Five Nights at Freddy's
Drawing with his favorite markers
And growing taller than his older cousin

May 18

She is the smell of fresh paint on canvas
The feel of dancing in the rain
The taste of strawberries straight from the plant
And the silence of the world while underwater
She is the stack of books that still need to be
read
The feeling of running through the grass right
before harvest
The smell of fresh chocolate chip cookies
And the twirl of a dress on the dance floor
She is made for collecting snow globes every
Christmas
Playing hockey throughout the winter
Midnight swims on an abandoned beach
And trying her best to be better than who she
used to be